Table of Contents

MW00809982

Foreword 5

Acknowledgements 7

The German Shorthaired Pointer.................................9

    Around The World 10

    The GSP as a Pet 11

    Pet Ownership 13

Breed History 15

    Versatile Hunting Dogs 16

    The United States..18

    The United Kingdom 19

    Australia & New Zealand 19

The Breed Standard 21

    General Appearance 21

    Size, Proportion, Substance 23

    Head..24

    Neck, Topline, Body 26

    Forequarters 27

    Hindquarters..28

    Coat..28

    Color...29

    Gait 30

    Temperament 31

Disqualifications..31

Color & The Black Issue..33

Re-introduction of the Color Black 33

Black in the USA...34

Colour Genetics..36

Docking & Dewclaw Removal 39

Why Dock?...39

The Movement to Ban Docking 39

The Versatile Hunting Dogs 43

Who Are They? 43

Differences Between the Breeds 45

The Similarities...46

The GSP In The Field 49

Introducing The Gun 53

Start Indoors 53

Moving it Outdoors 54

AKC Field Trials vs Hunt Tests 57

Field (Hunt) Tests 57

Field Trials 58

Deutsch Kurzhaars & The German Registry 61

The GSP As A Pet..65

Energy Levels 65

Children..66

Health & Maintenance..66

With Other Pets 67

Food 68

Grooming 71

Shedding 71

Ears 72

Nails 72

Training 75

Training Tips 75

Sit 77

Down 77

Heel 78

Come 78

Stay 79

Health Issues 81

Subaortic Stenosis 81

Hip Dysplasia 82

Eye Diseases 83

Lupoid Dermatosis (LD) 84

Hypothyroidism 84

Torn Cruciate 84

Cancer 84

Epilepsy 84

Separation Anxiety 85

Symptoms 85

Treating It 86

Finding A GSP Breeder 89

    Starting Your Search 90

    The Visit 92

Finding A Rescue Dog.. 95

Bringing Your Puppy Home 97

    Potty Training... 97

    Crate Training 98

    Pet Insurance 100

    Socialization 101

Dog Sports.. 103

    Agility 103

    Obedience... 104

    Dock Dogs 106

    Conformation.. 106

Breeding Your Dog & Puppy Development............................ 109

    Mentors 110

    Puppies at Birth 111

    The First Four Weeks 113

    From Four Weeks Onward 113

Photo Credits 117

Index 119

Resources... 123

    Reference Books 123

    Club Websites 123

Foreword

I have lived with German shorthaired pointers for almost twenty years. My first one came from a shelter and I fell madly in love with the breed. At the time I was breeding, showing and mushing Siberian Huskies. I knew I wanted to be just as involved with the GSP and so it began.

I love watching a GSP work a field even though I have no aspirations to hunt. The sheer athleticism of the breed is stunning in action. Whether you are someone who is just curious about the breed or looking to learn more in anticipation of getting one or learning more about the history behind the dog on your couch, I hope you find what you are looking for in this book.

I owe thanks to the many breeders and owners that sent me pictures of their dogs to use in this book. The credit for each photo is at the back of the book.

Thanks,
Heather

Acknowledgements

I would like to thank the many people that helped to create this guide by providing not only expert advice, but allowing me to add their amazing photos.

The German Shorthaired Pointer

The German shorthaired pointer, also known as the GSP or Deutsch Kurzhaar (DK), is a medium sized hunting breed that can be found in many countries around the world. They originated in Germany, where they remain a very popular dog for hunting, showing and as a pet.

Many breeds that were originally hunting dogs have split into two different types over the years – the show lines and the field lines. The two different types can be very different from one another and may not even be recognizable as the same breed in some cases. In the GSP, this split has not occurred. Good dogs often compete in both the field and the show ring and, while there can be some slight differences in appearance between some lines, all are easily identifiable as being German shorthaired pointers.

Around The World

This versatility in purpose, combined with his affable nature and handsome appearance, has made the breed very popular with hunters around the world. The GSP belongs to a group of dogs known as versatile hunting dogs. These dogs were bred to hunt fur and feather game on land and in the water. They need to be able to point game, retrieve it, and track it in the case of an injured animal. Other dogs that belong to this group include the German wirehaired pointer, vizsla, weimaraner, and the setters (English, Irish, Gordon, and Irish red and white).

Although there has been a trend to ban dog breeds over fears of aggression in many countries, the GSP is not and has never been banned anywhere. Although not nearly as popular as the Labrador and golden retrievers, the GSP has a firm following in Europe, Australia, North and South America. Although there are some GSP dogs in Asia and Africa, they have not gained the same degree of popularity yet as they have in other countries. They are especially common in countries where hunting is a popular pastime.

The GSP as a Pet

As a sporting breed that was bred to work in the field all day at a gallop, they should be expected to have a lot of stamina and energy. This can make them a difficult pet for those who are not active or do not have a means of allowing the dog to burn off that excessive energy. They excel in homes with runners, hikers, and other outdoor enthusiasts. They were always meant to work in close contact with the foot hunter and remain easy to train.

As a relatively healthy breed, the GSP suffers from fewer common genetic ailments than many other popular breeds. They live long lives, often reaching twelve to thirteen years of age, and tend to remain active and healthy throughout their senior years.

Depending on where you live, finding a German shorthaired pointer breeder may require going on a waiting list, although the list is rarely as long as it is for less common breeds. In some countries, rescued dogs are also available through re-homing groups such as shelters and rescue organizations. Unfortunately, there remains an element in the population that chooses to abandon a dog that won't hunt for them, by dumping the animal at the end of the hunting season.

Because he was bred to work closely with those unlikely to have more than one dog, the GSP often remained in the home and acted as both a protector and family companion. As a result, the GSP thrives on human contact and does not do well when left outdoors or in a kennel all the time. There is an old myth that dogs will hunt better if they are not treated as family pets. Unfortunately, some people still believe this. The German shorthaired pointer thrives on human contact and is happiest in the home, interacting with his family. Provided they are socialized with children, they tend to be patient with young ones and game for any adventure a child would like to undertake. Care does need to be taken to avoid having toddlers accidentally knocked over by an over-exuberant dog.

Pet Ownership

As with any pet, it is important to sit down and make sure that the breed is a good fit for your family's lifestyle. Ask yourself why you want a pet and how you will manage to meet his needs. A dog requires lots of time, training, and work. There are veterinary expenses as well as food and training expenses. In return, a dog will prove a most loyal companionship through thick and thin.

You will need to look into your local bylaws about dog ownership. Some municipalities put a limit on the number of pets that a person may have on the property and almost all will require that you purchase a license for your dog. If you rent your home, you will also need to make sure that your lease allows dogs and ensure that your dog does not disturb your neighbours if you live in an apartment or condominium type setting.

If you have young children, you should also be asking yourself if you have enough time to care for both the dog and the kids. Many people can manage both. Dogs and children can make an excellent combination, for some it can prove to be too much. All too often this is the reason a dog is given up to a shelter. Getting a dog without having the resources, including time, to care for it is unfair to the animal. Dropping him off at a shelter is confusing for the dog and can lead to separation anxiety due to a fear of abandonment.

All of these things should be considered before you ever begin to look for a dog. If, after careful consideration, you still feel you are ready to take on the responsibility of dog ownership, then welcome to that special group known as dog lovers.

"He is your friend, your partner, your defender, your dog. You are his life, his love, his leader. He will be yours, faithful and true, to the last beat of his heart. You owe it to him to be worthy of such devotion"
-- Unknown

Breed History

The beginnings of the German shorthaired pointer can be found in the 19th century. At the time, changes were occurring that allowed the common man to make use of some land for hunting game for

both sport and dinner. Prior to that, hunting with dogs was mainly conducted by noblemen and rich landowners. The latter could afford to have one dog to locate and point game, a spaniel to flush it up, and a retriever to bring it back to the hunter after it had been shot. They also had various types of hounds to find injured game or track fur bearing animals. The common man could not generally afford to feed so many dogs. He hunted mainly on foot and most of what he shot was destined for the dinner table. He needed one dog that could do all of those tasks. This is where the group of dogs known as versatile hunters began.

Versatile Hunting Dogs

The versatile hunting dog, a class to which the GSP belongs, should be able to locate game, point, flush it up for the gun, retrieve it to hand, track wounded animals, and do it on land and in the water. They should be able to work both feather and furred game. In essence, they needed to be a jack-of-all trades hunting dog that had enough stamina to work all day at a gallop over uneven ground. That is physically demanding and punishing work and requires good body structure to reduce the risk of injuries.

At the time these changes were happening, the most popular gun dog around was the Spanish pointer. This breed is at the base of many modern pointing breeds although few resemble the houndy ancestor seen in artwork at the time. The Germans added various other breeds to the mix to create what they viewed as the ideal dog for their hunting purposes. Although it is not clear exactly what breeds are included, it is commonly believed that there was some type of hound, most likely the Schweisshunde which should not be confused with the modern bloodhound, to give them trailing abilities. It is also likely that there is English pointer blood in the mix as well. The English pointer was prized for his scenting abilities and it is thought that he was added to the mix to improve the nose of the GSP. There may also have been some Setter added in as well.

The original dogs came in three colours – liver, black, and red. The liver colour was favoured by breeders and the other two colours gradually disappeared. The dogs were both solid in colouration and ticked with patches. The solid pattern was actually more popular in the early years of the breed's history. In the early part of the twentieth century, some breeders experimented with adding in more English pointer blood to further improve the breed's scenting abilities. The black dogs that came out of these breedings were registered as a sub-category of the GSP, known as Prussian shorthairs. Many years later in 1934, long after they had stopped adding in pointer blood to the GSP, an article was written noting that the dogs were different only in colour and that it was time to identify them for what they were – German shorthaired pointers. Shortly after the article came out, the Germans combined the two stud books and both colours have been registered as GSPs ever since. In Germany, as well as much of continental Europe, the GSP remains an all purpose hunting companion and is used on both fur and feathered game.

The United States

The GSP was not officially recognized with a written breed standard in the United States until 1946. Since that time the breed has gained in popularity as a hunting dog, pet, and show dog. In more recent years, as dog sports such as agility, flyball, dock dogs, and tracking have become more popular, the GSP's legion of fans has grown to include dog sport competitors. As a hunting dog, the GSP is mainly used on upland birds but they remain capable of hunting all types of game.

The United Kingdom

At about the same time as the GSP was becoming known in North America, it was also becoming more popular in the United Kingdom. Initially, there was high resistance post-World War II to anything that was German in origin. In addition to the prejudice, there was also the strict quarantine laws imposed on all incoming animals. This made importing a dog difficult and costly. The breed made slow headway but once people saw the versatility of the breed in the field it became increasingly popular. Today, GSPs are found throughout the British Isles. Versatile dogs in the U.K. are known as hunt point retrieve (HPR) dogs. Here too, they are mainly used on birds.

Australia & New Zealand

It took the breed a little longer to make its way to Australia and New Zealand. The combination of distance to travel, expense and quarantine requirements were daunting to many potential owners and breeders. Most of the original imports came from Britain. Once the foothold was gained, first in New Zealand and then in Australia, the breed became exceptionally popular. As in continental Europe, the Australians and New Zealanders made full use of the breed's hunting abilities with popular game including waterfowl, upland birds, rabbits, and deer. Today, the breed remains extremely popular in this part of the world.

The Breed Standard

A breed standard is a written description of the ideal specimen of the breed. It describes the features that make him look like his breed and able to do his original job. In the case of the German shorthaired pointer, this means that it describes a dog capable of hunting in the field all day at a gallop over uneven ground. It also describes the features that help separate the GSP from other pointing breeds with a similar colour. A good breeder knows his breed standard extremely well and uses it as his guideline when deciding on which puppy will carry his line forward to the next generation. Although newcomers to the sport of dogs may try to breed what is fashionable and winning in the conformation ring or field trials, a good breeder will always go back to the standard because breeding a correct dog is much more important than breeding a dog that wins a lot of ribbons and is crippled in his senior years.

Below, in bold, is the American Kennel Club (AKC) standard for the GSP. Comments and explanations are in italics.

General Appearance

The German Shorthaired Pointer is a versatile hunter, an all-purpose gun dog capable of high performance in field and water. The judgement of Shorthairs in the show ring reflects this basic characteristic. The overall picture which is created

in the observer's eye is that of an aristocratic, well balanced, symmetrical animal with conformation indicating power, endurance and agility and a look of intelligence and animation. The dog is neither unduly small nor conspicuously large. It gives the impression of medium size, but is like the proper hunter, "with a short back, but standing over plenty of ground." Symmetry and field quality are most essential. A dog in hard and lean field condition is not to be penalized; however, overly fat or poorly muscled dogs are to be penalized. A dog well balanced in all points is preferable to one with outstanding good qualities and defects. Grace of outline, clean-cut head, sloping shoulders, deep chest, powerful back, strong quarters, good bone composition, adequate muscle, well carried tail and taut coat produce a look of nobility and indicate a heritage of purposefully conducted breeding. Further evidence of this heritage is movement which is balanced, alertly coordinated and without wasted motion.

The general description section is meant to give an overview of the breed, emphasizing key points, and functional items. The general appearance section of the AKC standard is not substantially different from that of the Canadian Kennel Club (used in Canada), the Kennel Club (UK, Australia, New Zealand, Hong Kong, Singapore, and Malaysia), or the FCI standard (the rest of the world).

Size, Proportion, Substance

Size--height of dogs, measured at the withers, 23 to 25 inches. Height of bitches, measured at the withers, 21 to 23 inches. Deviations of one inch above or below the described heights are to be severely penalized. Weight of dogs 55 to 70 pounds. Weight of bitches 45 to 60 pounds. *Proportion*--measuring from the forechest to the rearmost projection of the rump and from the withers to the ground, the Shorthair is permissibly either square or slightly longer than he is tall. *Substance*--thin and fine bones are by no means desirable in a dog which must possess strength and be able to work over any type of terrain. The main importance is not laid so much on the size of bone, but rather on the bone being in proper proportion to the body. Bone structure too heavy or too light is a fault. Tall and leggy dogs, dogs which are ponderous because of excess substance, doggy bitches, and bitchy dogs are to be faulted.

The FCI standard is the only one which asks for a larger dog – both taller and heavier. All standards are looking for a dog that is square or slightly longer than tall. A dog that has bone structure that is too heavy is handicapped in terms of agility and stamina while a light boned dog may not have sufficient strength to do his job. If you have to err on one side or the other, slightly too fine is better than slightly too coarse. In general, the amount of bone should look appropriate for the size of the dog. Although not mentioned in the American standard, the dog should have slightly more length of leg than depth of body. This aids his ability to gallop all day.

Head

The *head* is clean-cut, is neither too light nor too heavy, and is in proper proportion to the body. The *eyes* are of medium size, full of intelligence and expression, good-humored and yet radiating energy, neither protruding nor sunken. The eye is almond shaped, not circular. The preferred color is dark brown. Light yellow eyes are not desirable and are a fault. Closely set eyes are to be faulted. China or wall eyes are to be disqualified. The *ears* are broad and set fairly high, lie flat and never hang away from the head. Their placement is just above eye level. The ears when laid in front without being pulled, should extend to the corner of the mouth. In the case of heavier dogs, the ears are correspondingly longer. Ears too long or fleshy are to be faulted. The *skull* is reasonably broad, arched on the side and slightly round on top. Unlike the Pointer, the median line between the eyes at the forehead is not too deep and the occipital bone is not very conspicuous. The foreface rises gradually from nose to forehead. The rise is more strongly pronounced in the dog than in the bitch. The jaw is powerful and the muscles well developed. The line to the forehead rises gradually and never has a definite stop as

24

that of the Pointer, but rather a stop-effect when viewed from the side, due to the position of the eyebrows. The *muzzle* is sufficiently long to enable the dog to seize game properly and be able to carry it for a long time. A pointed muzzle is not desirable. The depth is in the right proportion to the length, both in the muzzle and in the skull proper. The length of the muzzle should equal the length of skull. A dish-shaped muzzle is a fault. A definite Pointer stop is a serious fault. Too many wrinkles in the forehead is a fault. The *nose* is brown, the larger the better, and with nostrils well opened and broad. A spotted nose is not desirable. A flesh colored nose disqualifies. The chops fall away from the somewhat projecting nose. Lips are full and deep yet are never flewy. The *teeth* are strong and healthy. The molars intermesh properly. The bite is a true scissors bite. A perfect level bite is not desirable and must be penalized. Extreme overshot or undershot disqualifies.

The section on the skull is quite detailed with an emphasis on the characteristics that separate the GSP from his ancestral pointer and hound bloodlines. Most details are similar in all standards. The one notable difference is that the FCI standard prefers a Roman nose while the other standards tend to prefer that the top of the muzzle be flat. Despite this consistency, there is a wide range of skull types seen in the breed. Eastern European heads are houndier are on the whole with more flew and breadth than is typical in North America and elsewhere. The most variation is seen with North America. The skulls range from boxy to long provided that the length of skull equals the length of muzzle and there is sufficient muzzle to carry a large game bird, the skull type is acceptable.

Neck, Topline, Body

The *neck* is of proper length to permit the jaws reaching game to be retrieved, sloping downwards on beautifully curving lines. The nape is rather muscular, becoming gradually larger toward the shoulders. Moderate throatiness is permitted. The *skin* is close and tight. The *chest* in general gives the impression of depth rather than breadth; for all that, it is in correct proportion to the other parts of the body. The chest reaches down to the elbows, the ribs forming the thorax show a rib spring and are not flat or slabsided; they are not perfectly round or barrel-shaped. The back ribs reach well down. The circumference of the thorax immediately behind the elbows is smaller than that of the thorax about a hand's breadth behind elbows, so that the upper arm has room for movement. Tuck-up is apparent. The *back* is short, strong, and straight with a slight rise from the root of the tail to the withers. The loin is strong, is of moderate length, and is slightly arched. An excessively long, roached or swayed back must be penalized. The hips are broad with hip sockets wide apart and fall slightly toward the tail in a graceful curve. A steep croup is a fault. The *tail* is set high and firm, and must be docked, leaving approximately 40% of its length. The tail hangs down when the dog is quiet and is held horizontally when he is walking. The tail must never be curved over the back toward the head when the dog is moving. A tail curved or bent toward the head is to be severely penalized.

This description is typical of any working pointing breed. They need sufficient neck length to retrieve a bird from the ground, lots of chest depth and rib length to accommodate the heart and lungs, and a short loin to keep strength in the back when moving. A long back does not hold up over uneven ground as well and will ultimately tire the dog out more quickly.

Forequarters

The *shoulders* are sloping, movable, and well covered with muscle. The shoulder blades lie flat and are well laid back nearing a 45 degree angle. The upper arm (the bones between the shoulder and elbow joint) is as long as possible, standing away somewhat from the trunk so that the straight and closely muscled legs, when viewed from the front, appear to be parallel. Elbows which stand away from the body or are too close result in toes turning inwards or outwards and must be faulted. *Pasterns* are strong, short and nearly vertical with a slight spring. Loose, short-bladed or straight shoulders must be faulted. Knuckling over is to be faulted. Dewclaws on the forelegs may be removed. The *feet* are compact, close-knit and round to spoon-shaped. The toes are sufficiently arched and heavily nailed. The pads are strong, hard and thick.

A good front is essential to any dog that must have endurance. It will break down over time if it is not properly constructed leading to injuries and an inability to do the job they love well into their senior years. For breeders, a good front is one of the hardest aspects to breed into a dog and one of the easiest to lose.

Hindquarters

Thighs are strong and well muscled. Stifles are well bent. Hock joints are well angulated and strong with straight bone structure from hock to pad. Angulation of both stifle and hock joint is such as to achieve the optimal balance of drive and traction. Hocks turn neither in nor out. Cowhocked legs are a serious fault.

There is a tendency in some countries to produce excessive amounts of hindquarter angulation. The rear must be balanced with the front to provide endurance and stamina. An unbalanced dog will tire quickly.

Coat

The hair is short and thick and feels tough to the hand; it is somewhat longer on the underside of the tail and the back edges of the haunches. The hair is softer, thinner and shorter on the ears and the head. Any dog with long hair in the body coat is to be severely penalized.

Coat texture is often overlooked in the breed despite its importance to function. The German shorthaired pointer is expected to hunt in all types of weather, on land and in the water. They coat needs its dense texture to help protect the body in colder weather and in particular in cold water. A correctly texture coat will be difficult to wet down initially, the water will form beads on top of the coat until it is thoroughly doused.

Color

The coat may be of solid liver or a combination of liver and white such as liver and white ticked, liver patched and white ticked, or liver roan. A dog with any area of black, red, orange, lemon or tan, or a dog solid white will be disqualified.

As is discussed in later chapters, North America is the only part of the world where combinations of black and white and solid black are not considered as acceptable as these variations in the liver coat colour. The actual range of ticking can vary from almost solid white with a few patches of liver to a roan that is so heavily ticked it appears solid. The solid liver dogs are less popular in North America than elsewhere despite being an original colour pattern. They can be entirely solid liver or there may be patches of white with or without ticking.

Gait

A smooth lithe gait is essential. It is to be noted that as gait increases from the walk to a faster speed, the legs converge beneath the body. The tendency to single track is desirable. The forelegs reach well ahead as if to pull in the ground without giving the appearance of a hackney gait. The hindquarters drive the back legs smoothly and with great power.

A good gundog must be able to move well. Unbalanced or poor movement is indicative of structural faults that will impede him in the field.

Temperament

The Shorthair is friendly, intelligent, and willing to please. The first impression is that of a keen enthusiasm for work without indication of nervous or flightly character.

Disqualifications

China or wall eyes.
Flesh colored nose.
Extreme overshot or undershot.
A dog with any area of black, red, orange, lemon, or tan, or a dog solid white.

Color & The Black Issue

The breed originally came in three colours – liver (brown), black, and red. There were two basic coat patterns – the solid colour with or without patches of white, with or without ticking and the ticked and patched pattern which ranged from almost solid white with only a few patches of colour, to a heavily roaned dog that had so much ticking on it that it was hard to tell if it was ticked or solid. Over time, breeders showed a marked preference for the liver colour and the other two colours, whose genes are dominant to liver disappeared.

Re-introduction of the Color Black

At the beginning of the 19th century, some breeders added English pointer blood into their lines to improve scenting ability. The practise was only done for a very short period of time but it was successful in increasing the breed's air scenting skills. This reintroduced the colour black to the breed. For a time, the Germans registered the black dogs as Prussian shorthairs which they considered a sub-category of the breed. By 1934, the black dogs were no different in type than the liver dogs and an article appeared suggesting they should be treated no differently since they were all considered German shorthaired pointers. Shortly after that the

Germans combined the two stud books and the two colours have been treated equally ever since under the FCI breed standard.

Black in the USA

The breed was officially recognized by the American Kennel Club (AKC) in 1930 but it was 1946 before a written standard for the breed was drafted in the United States. Although the two stud books were separate in 1930, by 1946 they had been combined for some time. For reasons which many have guessed at but few have any real proof of, the Americans chose to only allow the liver colouration. They made black GSPs a disqualification in the show ring. Black dogs could (and still can) be registered by the AKC and compete in all types of performance events including field trials, field tests, obedience, and agility. The Canadians decided to make black a fault but not a disqualification. Despite it being a serious fault, there have been black and white Canadian conformation champions. The rest of the world accepts black on even footing with liver.

The issue of black GSPs remains a contentious one in North America where a growing group of breeders are doing their best to overturn the standard and make black acceptable in the show ring since it is acceptable in the country of origin (Germany). The United Kennel Club (UKC) which is smaller than the AKC but growing in size only uses country of origin breed standards and therefore allows black GSPs to compete in all events, including conformation.

Ironically, there have been many black GSPs imported to North America from Europe and other parts of the world that have made a substantial contribution to the breed in North America. Dogs such as the liver and white German born import KS Zobel v Pregelufer (a son of the influential black and white sire Ciro v Bichtelwald) can be found in the pedigrees of many well known North American kennels.

Colour Genetics

As mentioned above, the gene for black (B) is dominant to the gene for liver (b). This means that a liver coloured dog can only carry the genes for liver (bb). A black dog may carry two black genes (BB) or one black and one liver gene (Bb). So, if you breed two liver dogs together, you will only get liver coloured puppies. If you breed a black dog to a liver dog, you may get black dogs and liver dogs if the black dog also carries the liver gene. If the black dog does not carry the liver gene, the entire litter will be black.

The solid pattern is dominant to the patched and ticked pattern. So, two ticked dogs will never produce a solid liver dog. A solid liver dog bred to a ticked dog may produce both patterns provided that they carry the gene for the ticked pattern.

Docking & Dewclaw Removal

Why Dock?

The German shorthaired pointer is a breed that traditionally has a docked tail and has had their dewclaws removed. The reasoning behind this was that the GSP ran through heavy ground cover and was prone to tearing their dewclaws off if they got caught on some of the undergrowth. So, to prevent an injury that tends to bleed heavily while afield, the dewclaws were removed shortly after birth. This practise was and is done in many breeds to protect them from torn nail beds. The tail was also docked for protective reasons. When you see a GSP in the field searching for birds you will notice the frantic wagging of the tail. In heavy cover and areas with many trees, the tail would break if it struck a tree. Similarly, if the tail received a cut or wound, the injury would re-open each time the tail struck something. This made it very difficult to get the wound to heal.

The Movement to Ban Docking

In recent years there has been a push by many animal rights groups to put a stop to docking. Most groups leave dewclaw removal alone which is ironic in that the two are done in the same basic manner and one procedure is no more traumatic to the puppy than the other. In some countries, such as Sweden, and in parts of Australia, bans against docking have been enacted into law. In many of these countries hunting is not common. In countries that have begun banning the practise of docking and where hunting is common, there has been a corresponding increase in tail injuries. Some countries, such as the United Kingdom, have recognized that a working dog needs to be docked in this breed. They allow legal docking of dogs that will be placed in hunting homes. These dogs may not be shown at some shows, although they can be shown at others.

The problem arises in the timing of docking. It is usually done within a few days of birth, at which point there is no way of knowing which puppy will be sold to a working home and which will go to a pet home. In the U.K., breeders tend to decide upon the whole litter at birth and then find the homes that will work best for the decision they made. Docking at a later age would be traumatic and painful for the dog who would have already adjusted to having a tail as part of his natural balance. Waiting to make a decision about whether a specific dog will be docked until he is older is cruel.

Many breeders find that docking bothers them far more than it does the puppy, who may cry for a few minutes and then return to what he was doing. Anyone who has had to deal with the docking of an adult dog due to injury will tell you it is very painful and a difficult adjustment for the dog. The goal of responsible breeders that dock their GSPs is to prevent injury in the field. Many German shorthaired pointers hunt routinely in their new homes as hunting remains a popular pastime in North America.

The Versatile Hunting Dogs

Versatile hunting dogs are dogs that are meant to do many different jobs in the field. They locate game, point it, flush it (if desired), retrieve it, and even track it. They are meant to be able to hunt both birds and furred game on land and in the water. In essence they were created to work for a man who could not afford or did not want to have multiple dogs. These dogs were developed in a number of different countries including Germany, Hungary, Italy, Holland, Ireland, England, Scotland and France.

Who Are They?

The following breeds are considered to be versatile hunting dogs, as accepted by the North American Versatile Hunting Dog Association (NAVDHA):

English Pointer (England)

English Setter (England)

German Shorthaired Pointer (Germany)

German Longhaired Pointer (Germany)

German Wirehaired Pointer (Germany)

Weimaraner (Germany)

Large Munsterlander (Germany)

Small Munsterlander (Germany)

Pudelpointer (Germany)

Stichelhaar (Germany)

Slovakian Wirehaired Pointer (Slovakia)

Portuguese Pointer (Portugal)

Vizsla (Hungary)

Wirehaired Pointing Griffon (Holland)

Drentsche Patrijshond (Holland)

Blue Picardy Spaniel (France)

Brittany Spaniel (France)

Braque Bourbonnais (France)

French Spaniel (France)

Braque Français (France)

Braque D'Auvergne (France)

Cesky Fousek (Czech Republic)

Irish Setter (Ireland)

Irish Red & White Setter (Ireland)

Gordon Setter (Scotland)

Italian Spinone (Italy)

Bracco Italiano (Italy)

Many of these breeds are relatively rare outside their country of origin. NAVHDA is a North American organization that grew out of desire by hunters to maintain the full skill range of these breeds despite the fact that in North America they are mainly used on upland birds.

Differences Between the Breeds

They were developed in a variety of regions partially because of the differences in the terrain that they hunted. For example, the Italian Spinone looks quite different from many of the other pointing breeds in terms of structure because he was developed to work in the Piedmont Mountains of Italy while most of the other breeds were meant for flat, uneven ground.

When you watch the different breeds in the field, you will notice different styles of running, quartering the field, and even pointing. All are fairly adaptable to any type of terrain as a key aspect of their versatility, but they do tend to shine in some situations better than others. The German shorthaired pointer tends to be a fast moving dog that runs at a gallop in the field while quartering. They range out but generally stay within sight of the hunter. The Brittany tends to range much further out, while the bracco Italiano tends to stay closer to the hunter. The Italian Spinone actually checks back with the hunter while on point since the rough terrain meant the hunter often wanted the dog to flush the bird up rather than wait for the hunter to reach him.

The Similarities

The GSP is one of the most popular of the versatile hunters and one of the breeds that has the least divergence between field and show lines. Brittanies and vizslas often have very little divergence as well. Setters tend to almost be two separate breeds when you compare the field lines to the show lines even differing in size.

In terms of general shape and structure, most of the breeds tend to be square or slightly longer than tall. There is an emphasis on a long muzzle with good scenting abilities and the structure to support endurance, power, and stamina. Almost all of them are high energy dogs. The coats vary greatly from the shorthaired dogs like the GSP, smooth vizsla, and weimaraner to the medium length coats like that of the Brittany spaniel to the long coated dogs such as the setter breeds. There are also wirehaired breeds like the German wirehaired, the wirehaired pointing griffon, and the wirehaired vizsla. Ticking is common in the coats of many of them as is solid colours in liver and other colours. Most of them share common ancestors.

NAVHDA and their hunting tests and titles tend to be held in high regard as they require the dog to demonstrate all aspects of versatility. Most hunt tests and trials focus on the pointing and retrieving aspects and ignore the tracking abilities of these breeds.

The GSP In The Field

The GSP in an intense dog in the field, often quivering with excitement when on point. Pet owners will notice their dogs naturally pointing from a young age at everything from butterflies to songbirds. Pointing is instinctive. In the field though, training becomes as important as instinct. Pointing is instinctive but holding point and waiting for the hunter to arrive is a result of training.

When hunting, the dog will quarter the field. This means he moves across it in a back and forth pattern than allows him to scent the entire field. He does this at a reasonable speed, usually while galloping. Some dogs will have a good natural pattern while others dogs will need to be trained.

Game is scented in the air and the nose is pointed upwards to catch eddies of game scent. You can tell when the dog has caught the scent of something since they tend to hone in on it and break pattern to follow the scent. Depending on wind conditions, it can be difficult to locate the precise position of the game. The dog may reposition himself several times and end up almost on top of it before finding the exact spot. Other times, they may point from quite a distance.

Once on point the dog should hold it staunchly while waiting for the hunter. They can follow a running bird with their eyes but should not move from their position. Depending on hunting style, the hunter may flush up the bird himself or have the dog do it for him. For the safety of the animal, the dog must hold position once the bird takes flight and is shot. The dog will watch where the bird falls and mark its location. The hunter will then send the dog to retrieve the bird to his hand. If the bird was injured but not killed, the dog may need to track it as it may have run when it fell from the air. The mouth is sufficiently gentle that a wounded bird may still be alive when it is dropped into the hunter's hand.

While some behaviors will occur naturally, it is training that elevates a truly great gun dog. They must work closely with the hunter. For many hunters, the partnership with the dog brings great pleasure and the day in the field is as enjoyable because of the time spent pursuing game as it is for successfully bringing it home.

In North America, the American Kennel Club (AKC) and Canadian Kennel Club (CKC) offer hunt tests and field trials to demonstrate the working abilities of the dogs. These focus on the animal's ability to locate game, point it, be steady to wing and shot (in these tests the dog is not allowed to flush the game up), and retrieve to hand. At the highest levels they must also demonstrate an ability to retrieve game downed over the water.

Introducing The Gun

Gunshyness is one of the most common problems found in sporting dogs and it is completely man-made as a general rule. It almost always stems from bad experiences with loud noises and a poor introduction to the sound of gunfire. You should never just bring a dog out to the field and shoot over him. Introducing your dog to the gun is not necessary if you do not intend to hunt over him. However, introducing him to loud noises can help alleviate stress during events like fireworks.

Start Indoors

Start when your puppy is little. While he is eating you can "accidentally" drop the occasional pot or pan than makes a loud racket. Eating is a pleasurable action for him and the goal is to make the noise less distracting because it occurs during a fun period of time. It is normal for the puppy to be startled the first time; he should return to his food or move to explore the pot within a few seconds. If he is very shaken by the experience, wait a few days and then repeat the action only this time do it in another room that is further away so that the sound is more muffled. Repeat the action a few days apart until your puppy is unfazed by the noise.

Moving it Outdoors

The next step is to move out to the field, this need not be done if you do not intend to hunt over the dog. It is easiest to do it if you have someone helping you. Plant some birds for your puppy. Pick a species that is small and fairly gentle such as pigeons or quail. Send your friend out about 75 yards away with a .22 crimp or starter's pistol. Let your puppy go in the direction of the birds. The goal is to let him flush them up so don't worry about pointing. Once he flushes a bird up and is chasing it in a direction other than towards your friend, lift your arm to let your friend know he should fire the gun. Ideally, when the gun goes off your puppy is having so much fun chasing the birds that he doesn't even notice the sound. If he is alarmed, put the gun away and spend some time playing in the field with him and the birds. Wait at least a week before trying it again, this time with your friend further away. Once he is unfazed by the firing of the gun at a distance, you can try it again with your friend about 10-15 yards closer. Repeat the exercise.

Continue this process until your friend is firing the gun fairly close to the action and your dog is not bothered. If a distance bothers your dog, back up a step by increasing the distance and repeating it until he is comfortable with it. Once your dog is good with the starter's pistol being fired fairly close to him, send your friend back out to the 75 yard distance but this time give him a .22 blank (which is louder). Repeat the process again. Once he is completely unfazed by the .22 blank you can move on to your quietest shotgun, etc until your dog is not bothered by your 12 gauge.

If you have followed the steps carefully, you will have a dog that associates the sound of the gun with birds flying.

AKC Field Trials vs Hunt Tests

For those interested in doing field work and earning titles through the American Kennel Club's testing and trial program, there are two different options. Hunt tests are a non-competitive venue where the dog's performance is judged against a standard and he earns a score which may or may not be a passing score. In field trials, the dogs compete against one another in pairs for finds and they are scored by judges on things like style, number of finds, speed, etc. The focus of hunt tests is somewhat different than that of field trials. Dogs can be successful in both venues although most are better at one than the other.

Field (Hunt) Tests

The German shorthaired pointer was developed for the foot hunter and the hunt tests come closer to his original function. They are judged on things like handler control, pattern, pace, pointing ability, retrieve, and desire to hunt. They are judged against a standard rather than one another. So, many dogs may achieve a passing score at a test. There are three testing levels in the United States – Junior Hunter (JH) which is looking for basic skills, Senior Hunter (SH) which is more advanced and requires that the dog retrieve and be steady to shot, and Master Hunter (MH) which requires that the dog be steady to wing and shot, retrieve to hand, and honor their bracemate (a second dog that runs concurrently). There are separate tests that dogs of all levels can complete that test water retrieving ability. In Canada, the water retrieve is built into the highest level – Field Dog Excellent (FDX), which is otherwise similar to the Master Hunter test.

Field Trials

Field trials are competitive and there is a winner and up to four placements. Judges may also single out other deserving dogs for recognition. Dogs compete in braces and the handler and judge are usually on horseback. There are walking trials but they are significantly less common than horseback trials. There are different stakes (classes) that dogs can run in. They range from the basic puppy and derby stakes to the gun dog and all ages stakes. Gun dog stakes are geared towards a dog that checks in with the hunter more often and tends to stay within eyesight. All ages dogs range further and are frequently expected to range beyond eyesight and hunt independently, holding point until the judge and handler find them. The judges are looking for a finished dog that has a brisk, energetic running style, covers lots of ground, point, is steady to wing and shot, and retrieves to hand.

Both can be very enjoyable sports to do with your dog. Field trialers tend to want a bigger running dog than many foot hunters do. If you intend to field trial your dog, you may be better off going to a breeder who breeds specifically for field dog trials.

Deutsch Kurzhaars & The German Registry

The breed originated in Germany and the Germans are one of the few national clubs that exert any control over the breeding practises of dogs in that country. This is true of all purebred dogs bred in Germany. In that country they have people known as breed wardens for each breed. This person must approve all dogs as being of breeding quality in order for any of their offspring to be able to be registered in Germany.

This is a very different system from that of North America or most of the rest of the world where the decision as to if a dog is of breeding quality is completely come up to the owner. To be declared to be good for breeding, a dog must pass a conformation evaluation and also a series of field tests. While the dogs look slightly different in Germany due to the fact they are often larger and coarser than what is typically seen in North America. In order to become a champion in Germany the dog must have field and show titles.

The German name for the German shorthaired pointer is the Deutsch Kurzhaar, often shortened in North America to DK. Unlike every other registry in the world, the Germans will only register DKs that are born in Germany or come out of German registered parents. This means that an AKC registered dog that is born in the United States out of North American bloodlines cannot be registered in the German system. This makes it very exclusive

too. Some hunters feel the DKs, as they are often referred to in North America, are better hunting dogs with more intensity. They import DKs from other countries and then breed them to other

DKs in the USA or other country. They register their dogs in the German system and run German tests in North America so their dogs can qualify for breeding under the German registry.

Some people believe that the DK is basically a different breed because the Germans have so many regulations in place that is basically a closed system. Others feel that they are all basically the same dog and that since you cannot tell a DK from any other German shorthaired pointer without looking up their pedigree and registration, it is foolish to consider them separate despite the restrictions the Germans place on breeding practises.

The GSP As A Pet

The German shorthaired pointer can make an excellent family pet. They do not require much grooming and are easily trained. Most GSPs respond to positive training methods and learn quickly. They are a breed that wants to please his family, making them easy to work with and train.

Energy Levels

For most families the biggest drawback will be the amount of exercise needed to keep the dog happy. The GSP is a very energetic breed and requires lots of daily exercise. Rural homes with acreage may not find this difficult to accommodate, but city dwellers that work all day would be advised to consider locating nearby dog parks and areas where their dog can run on a regular basis. Signing your pet up for activities like doggy daycare and canine hiking may also be helpful, particularly in the younger years.

For those who run or jog, the GSP can be an ideal running companion. If the dog has been trained to respond well when off leash and you enjoy running on nature trails that allow off-leash dogs, your GSP will gladly cover twice as much ground as you do.

Training is important. The GSP puppy is perfectly capable of beginning basic training as soon as he arrives at your home.

Remember that what is cute as a small puppy isn't nearly as cute when the dog weighs 60 pounds. The adult GSP weighs between 50 and 70 pounds and is 21 to 25 inches tall at the shoulder. They are strong, athletic dogs and must be trained or you will spend a lot of time with a sore shoulder from holding the leash and experience a lot of frustration.

Children

The German shorthaired pointer is generally a good dog with children. It is important to socialize them with children and to always supervise the two together. Regardless of breed or personality of the dog, no dog should ever be left unsupervised with young children. Accidents can happen very easily and a dog has no way to communicate his discomfort or pain besides growling or snapping. Children cannot be counted on to read a dog's body language and understand that the animal's patience has come to its end. That is the adult's job. Regardless - it is understandable if a dog bites when repeatedly provoked, it is the dog that will pay the ultimate price. Do yourself and your pet a favour and never leave him unsupervised with children.

Health & Maintenance

Grooming requirements are minimal and they are generally a long-lived, healthy breed. As mentioned earlier, the typical lifespan is twelve or more years. Although there are a few illnesses associated with the breed, there are far fewer than many other breeds of dog and they tend to age well, remaining active and healthy for most of their lives.

With Other Pets

In terms of how they are with other animals, much depends on how they are introduced and the individual dog. Most GSPs are fairly playful and are keen to play with other dogs. If you are adding a GSP and already have an existing dog, it is best to make sure your first dog is at least a year and preferably two years old. Having your first dog be at least a year or two older will automatically put him in the dominant position and avoid having dominance issues later in life. It is best that your second dog be of the opposite sex to your first dog, provided that both have been fixed. This too helps avoid dominance issues. If you must have two dogs of the same sex, two males are generally better than two females. Introduce your new pet to your other dog on neutral territory such as a local park and then bring them home together.

Some German shorthaired pointers love cats and you will find the two sleeping side by side. Others will chase the cat and may even kill it. It is very important to ensure that the dog understands that the cat is a member of the family and not to be chased. With a puppy this is not that hard to do but it can be more difficult when you adopt an adult dog. Always keep the dog on a leash around the cat until you are sure of their reaction and do not leave the two together unsupervised until you are very certain that they will get along.

It is not advisable to have a German shorthaired pointer loose with small rodent type pets. The prey instinct is likely to kick in and create chaos at best and, at worst, a dead rodent.

Food

Most GSPs will thrive on a good commercial dog food. Food allergies do occur occasionally, but not nearly as often as they do in breeds like Labrador retrievers. You can also choose a raw or homemade diet for your dog. If you choose to go the raw or homemade route, it is very important that you ensure that the diet is completely balanced for your dog. This may involve consulting a canine nutritionist. An unbalanced diet can lead to nutritional problems including malnutrition, vitamin deficiencies and poisoning from vitamin build up in the body. Maintaining your dog in good muscle tone and at a healthy weight will help ensure that he lives a long and healthy life. Most GSPs are chow-hounds and free feeding is generally inadvisable with this breed.

Like people, dogs are all individuals and there are unique personality differences in each one. Common personality traits include goofiness and playfulness, fun-loving, energetic, and affectionate. Most GSPs think they are lap dogs throughout their lives.

Grooming

In terms of grooming, the German shorthaired pointer is relatively low maintenance. The short coat does not mat, attract burs, or do anything else but get muddy. It does shed though. Because the hairs are short and often dark, they are not as noticeable as the longer hairs of a retriever or other breeds but they are very noticeable when you sweep your floors. They are also quite evident if you are wearing a light coloured suit and your dark dog rubs against it. The texture of the hairs is such that they tend to poke into fabrics and stick to them.

Shedding

To cut down on shedding, try using a hound glove to brush your dog down once a week. A hound glove has small rubber nubs on it and is good at removing loose, dead hair from the coat. Bathing should not be done too frequently as you do not want to strip the natural oils from the coat. With the exception of adventures of the smelly kind, you should only need to bathe your GSP a few times a year.

Ears

The German shorthaired pointer has a drop ear which means that at least part of the time, the ear flap is covering the ear canal. Because the ear of the GSP is not as hairy as that of a spaniel or retriever, it is less prone to infection. You should make a point of cleaning your dog's ears out once a month as a preventative measure. It is easy to do and many dogs actually enjoy the feeling. Use baby wipes to clean the ears; they are hygienic and meant for delicate skin. Wrap a portion of the wipe around your index finger. The adult person's index finger is big enough that you are unlikely to be able to get too deep into the ear canal. If you have exceptionally small hand or your dog is unusually large, avoid going too deep. Wipe down the grooves of the ear canal and make sure you get the dirt out. There should not be any unusual odor. That would be a sign of infection. While ear infections are uncommon in most individuals, your veterinarian can prescribe antibiotic ear drops that can easily treat most infections.

Nails

The toe nails of the GSP are generally thick and hard. They also grow quickly on many dogs. Depending on the types of surfaces your dog walks on, he may wear them down naturally. If he does not, you will need to clip his nails regularly. For some, it needs to be done on a weekly basis. You can cut them using traditional canine nail clippers or you can use a dremel-type tool to grind them down. Many owners find the latter easier to use but it is a matter of personal preference.

The nails of the GSP are often black, making it difficult to see the vein that runs down the center which is called the quick. You do not want to cut the quick as it is quite painful for your dog and it tends to bleed excessively. Start by trimming or grinding a small amount off the end of the nail. If you stay on top of your dog's nail trimming routine, you will only ever have to take off the tips. If you look at the nail from the bottom you can see the beginnings of the quick in the center of the nail – it looks slightly lighter in colour. If you do accidentally cut the quick, apply pressure and use a styptic powder to stop the bleeding. If you let the nails get too long, it will be uncomfortable for your dog and they will interfere with how your pet walks, eventually causing a problem.

Training

All dogs should be trained and it should begin as soon as your dog arrives in your home. The GSP tends to be very food and praise motivated and learns quickly and easily. It is important to decide upon the house rules before your new pet arrives. Everyone in the household must agree to abide by and enforce those rules. It is very confusing for your dog if you don't allow him on the furniture and your spouse does. It just makes it harder for him to learn the rules. Staying calm, being patient and being consistent are the key aspects of successful training.

Training Tips

When training a puppy, it is better to do short sessions frequently rather than one long session. A puppy has a short attention span and you want to keep training sessions fun for both of you. Consider taking a puppy obedience or socialization class with your dog. It can be a good bonding experience and also exposes your dog to other animals. Best of all, it allows a trainer to help you catch problems before they become more serious.

Vary your rewards so that they are not always food rewards. Sometimes it can be a game of tug or an ear rub or some other gesture of affection. Dogs appreciate all of these and it helps ensure that you don't end up with a dog that only listens to you if you have food in your hand.

Training on a leash initially until a command is known will help you control your dog's actions and keep his focus on you. Begin training in an area with as few distractions as possible so that he stays focussed on you.

Modern trainers mostly focus on positive training methods. This works well with the German shorthaired pointer. Most respond well to the tone of your voice and thrive on your spending time with them. Harsh methods can lead to the dog shutting down and refusing to do anything at all. Clicker training, which uses a small tool called a clicker to allow more precise shaping of behavior can be very successful in training GSPs.

Always end your training sessions on a positive note. If you feel yourself becoming frustrated or angry, it is time to return to a command that your dog knows well such as sit. Give the command, the dog obeys, you reward and then end the session. The German shorthaired pointer is very sensitive to tone of voice and as you become more frustrated and your tone changes, so too will your dog's behavior and likely not for the better. Training needs to be enjoyable for both of you and it should always end on a positive note.

Sit

Sit is the first command you should teach your dog and one of the easiest ones for a puppy to master. Your dog's leash should not be tight but it should be taut enough that he cannot back away. Taking a treat, hold it just above his nose. Once you have his attention, give the command and gradually move the treat towards the back of his head. He will have to sit down to follow the treat. As soon as he does, praise and reward him. Do not attempt to push his bum down as he may misinterpret this and even work to avoid the pressure from your hand.

Down

Put your dog in a sit. Again, hold the leash tight enough that he cannot back up. Holding the treat in front his nose, give the command and slowly lower it to between his front legs. His bum will slide out and he will go into a down in order to follow the treat. As soon as he does, praise and reward him.

Heel

The GSP is a strong dog and having one yank you down the street is very uncomfortable. Teaching your dog to heel or walk without pulling you along is essential. Start while he is young. Exit the house and put him in a sit. Give the command and begin walking. As soon as your dog begins to pull on the leash, stop. Do not move until he comes back and the lead is again loose. Then give the command and begin walking again. As soon as he pulls on the leash, stop again. Repeat this until he gets the idea. The first few times it can take forever to get out of the driveway but he will quickly get the idea that if he pulls, he won't get to go anywhere.

Come

Start in a small room with you sitting on the floor and the puppy on a loose leash. Call him to you. As soon as he comes, praise and reward him lavishly. If he ignores you, give the lead a gentle tug to get his attention and repeat the command. You may need to use the lead to bring him to you. It is important that he realizes that this is a non-negotiable command and that he must come when called. It could save his life one day. Once he is coming reliably, extend the leash a bit more. Gradually add in distractions and move from indoors to outdoors. You can buy extra-long leads for training that are twenty feet or more long. He has to come when called, and he should never be off leash until he has a good recall. When it is finally time to try it without a leash, make sure you are in a fenced in area for safety reasons. Always give the command in a friendly voice. Do not repeat it multiple times and do not yell. No dog is going to want to come to someone who seems angry. If he doesn't come, use the leash to begin bringing him to you. As soon as he begins doing it on his own make sure that you praise and reward him heavily.

Stay

This is one of the hardest commands for your dog to learn as his natural tendency is to move towards you. Put him in a sit position and stand directly in front of him. Give the command and take a single, small step backwards. Only hold it for a few seconds and then praise and reward him. Gradually increase the length of time you have him hold his position at that distance until he is staying reliably for a few minutes. If he moves towards you, go back to him put him in a stay and try it again with less wait time. You can now increase the distance by another step. Begin with short wait times again and gradually lengthen them. Gradually increase the distance again and repeat. Eventually you should be able to walk away from him and have him stay for several minutes.

Health Issues

On the whole, the German shorthaired pointer is a healthy breed. Since they typically live twelve or more years with many reaching fourteen or fifteen years of age. Some even making it past that. There are certain tests your breeder should have done on the parents of your puppy before they were bred. They include cardiac certification, hip x-rays, eye certification, and cone degeneration. All of these are once in a lifetime tests except the eye certification which must be done annually. Many breeders are now also doing elbow x-rays, thyroid testing and von Willebrands (a bleeding disorder) tests as well. All three of these are for very rare problems in the breed but testing certainly doesn't hurt.

It is important to note that the genetic inheritance of many diseases involves numerous genes and can be very complicated. While testing significantly reduces the likelihood that your dog will not get sick, it is still a possibility.

Subaortic Stenosis: This is a heart condition that occurs occasionally in the breed. It is a narrowing of the area just below the aortic valve. It often presents as a heart murmur. It should not be confused with the mild heart murmurs often present in puppies that disappear as they age. There are degrees of severity and a dog with a mild stenosis will likely never be bothered by symptoms of the disease but should not be bred. A severe stenosis can present as exercise intolerance, fainting, arrhythmias, and general fatigue. Medication may help but the disease will likely shorten the dog's lifespan. Severe stenosis is very rare in the breed and the national club is determined to keep it that way by making it a strongly suggested test for all dogs used in breeding programs.

Hip Dysplasia: Although hip dysplasia occurs in the breed, it is not nearly as common as it is in many similar sized breeds such as Labrador and golden retrievers. Hip dysplasia involves poor placement of the bones in the hip joint leading to degeneration and arthritis at a younger than expected age. In severe cases, surgery may be recommended. Dogs should be x-rayed for hip dysplasia after the age of two years old for Orthopedic Foundation for Animals (OFA) certification. PennHIP is an alternative program that can be done at any age. A veterinarian must be specially trained to offer PennHIP certification x-rays. Elbow dysplasia is extremely rare in the breed however many vets are now offering to x-ray elbows for a very minimal charge at the same time as they do hips so it is becoming increasingly common for breeders to do both hips and elbows.

Eye Diseases: The most common eye issue in the GSP is cataracts. Because many diseases develop as a dog ages, eye certification must be done annually by a veterinary ophthalmologist. Other diseases known to occur include retinal folds (no vision consequences) and retinal detachment (causes blindness). The German shorthaired pointer is also one of the breeds that have cone degeneration (CD – also known as dayblindness). There is a gene test for CD since it is a simple one gene controlled diseases. Dogs tested clear can never produce any affected offspring. Dogs that are carriers should only be bred to non-carriers/clear dogs to avoid producing affected puppies. Affected dogs should obviously not be bred at all but if they were bred to a non-carrier, they would only produce carriers.

Lupoid Dermatosis (LD): LD is a skin disorder that is characterized by open, crusty sores and severe inflammation. There is no known cure. A gene test has been developed but the results are currently indicating that the inheritance of the disease may not be as simple as originally expected. As a result, many breeders are not testing until the whole story about inheritance is better understood.

Hypothyroidism: Hypothyroidism does occur in the breed, often later in life. Dogs often gain weight, develop a voracious appetite, and may lose patches of hair. Hypothyroidism is diagnosed by a blood test and treated with medication.

Torn Cruciate: Cruciate injuries often occur in this breed, particularly later in life. They tend to run at high speeds over uneven ground making them vulnerable to ligament tears and injuries when they put a foot in a hole while running. Most cruciate injuries are treated with surgery and a long recovery period.

Cancer: Although cancer does occur occasionally at a young age, most deaths from cancer are at an advanced age. Cancer is very often the cause of death though.

Epilepsy: Epilepsy does occur in the GSP and unfortunately, there are no tests for it and no real understanding of its pattern of inheritance.

Separation Anxiety

German shorthaired pointers, like many pointing breeds, are meant to work closely with people and tend to bond very tightly to their family. When they change home due to circumstances beyond their control, it can be quite traumatic. If they end up spending time in a shelter, it makes it worse. Unfortunately, shelters tend to be understaffed and there just isn't enough time to give each dog the one-on-one attention they need. This can lead to the development of a disorder known as separation anxiety.

Dogs can develop it for a variety of reasons and some breeds are more prone to it than others. Time in a shelter with less one-on-one time than the dog is used to can definitely cause it, but so can sudden changes in lifestyle, the loss of a family member, moving residences, and other traumatic changes. It can be anything from mild to really severe. In essence, it is a fear of abandonment and being alone that leads to panic.

Symptoms

Common symptoms of a dog that is suffering from mild separation anxiety include clinginess and anxiety when you are leaving the house. The dog may bark and cry excessively. When you return they may have soiled themselves, drooled a lot, and there may be signs that they were trying to get out of their crate. Dogs left alone in house may become extremely destructive, chewing door knobs and door frames in their attempt to follow you. Dogs with severe separation anxiety should not be crated since they can hurt themselves in their attempts to get out of the crate. If at all possible, try to create a safe space where they can stay without hurting them or utterly destroying the room.

Treating It

The goal is to desensitize and reassure the dog that all is well. It is a disease that is best tackled by working with a professional animal behaviorist and your veterinarian. They can help you draw up a plan to work towards readjusting your dog and getting them past it. Common suggestions for mild separation anxiety include leaving clothing items that smell like you (that you no longer want) with the dog to help reassure him. You can also leave the television or a radio on so that your dog does not feel as alone. Avoid making a big deal out of leaving. Your dog watches you get ready to go and knows what it means when you put him in is crate with a special toy. Instead tuck him away a bit before you intend to leave so he doesn't know that it immediately means you're leaving. When you come home, take the time to take your coat off and take a few minutes before you greet your dog. Do not make a big fuss over him.

Getting a dog over separation anxiety can be a long process. It often starts with very short absences and the increase can be very slow. It can be frustrating and difficult. It is important to remember that your dog is not behaving like this to spite you. He is genuinely terrified when you leave. Consulting an animal behaviorist and your veterinarian can be helpful not only in finding ways to help your dog but also in finding encouragement for yourself that there are ways to handle the problem.

Finding A GSP Breeder

When you decide you want to get a German shorthaired pointer, you have two basic choices. You can get your dog from a breeder or adopt one from a shelter or rescue group. In the next chapter, you will learn how to find a rescue dog. In this one, you will learn about how to differentiate between a good, responsible breeder and someone who is only breeding their dog to make some extra cash.

When you breed dogs properly, you are lucky to break even. The expenses of raising the female including normal veterinary expenses, doing all the health checks, competing with her, the stud fee, whelping the litter and raising it, registering it, vaccinating it, and microchipping or tattooing it; it all adds up to a tidy sum even if nothing goes wrong. If something goes wrong, it can get very expensive very fast.

Starting Your Search

Start your search for a breeder with the national club in your country. They often have a list of breeders in the country that have signed a code of ethics. This is not a guarantee of quality and you do still have to do your research but it is a good place to start. Sit down and make a list of the questions you want to ask the breeders before you begin contacting them. It is easy to forget things during the actual conversation so have your list on hand.

You should be looking for the following:

- Written bill of sale and contract
- Genetic health guarantee?
- What health tests do they do on their dogs?
- What activities do they do with their dogs?

Everything should be in writing. A good breeder has faith in the quality of their dogs and is willing to back it up in writing. The health guarantee should also be in writing. A health guarantee should outline what happens if your pet develops a genetic illness that prevents them from living a normal life. It usually indicates if they will offer a refund or a replacement puppy when the next one becomes available. It should last at least two years and preferably five or more. Many diseases will not show up until the dog is at least a year or two old. It can take longer in some cases. A breeder who does the recommended test for their breed – in this case, eyes, heart and hip certifications and CD gene testing – will have diminished the odds as much as possible and be willing to take responsibility if something does go wrong. It is not enough to ask about health certificates; you should be able to see proof that they have been done.

Although not every dog enjoys being a show dog or hunting, the breeder should do things with their dogs generally. A third party's evaluation of the dog in the field or the conformation ring does count for something. An experienced breeder can tell a good dog from bad but everyone can develop kennel blindness and fail to see the faults in their own dogs. While there does not need to be a title on every dog and some of the most successful producing dogs have never become champions in the field or the ring, there should still be a record of showing their dogs or working their dogs in the field, and preferably both, as a general rule.

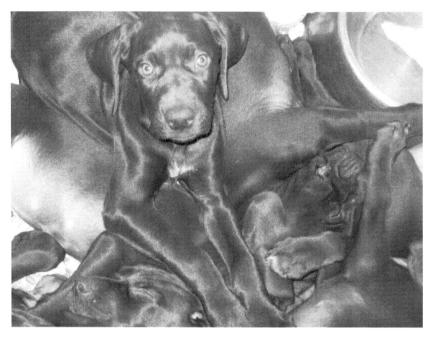

Expect the breeder to have questions for you too. They should be interested in what kind of home you would provide for their puppy. They want to know if your lifestyle is suitable to the breed and that you are committed to giving the dog the best possible home.

The Visit

Set up times to visit the breeders that interest you whenever possible. Meeting people in person is better than relying on phone calls and emails. The images on the computer are not always the same as reality. When you visit, you should remember that it is significantly harder to keep clean floors when you have multiple dogs running across your floors, especially if its muddy outside. Having said that, it should be reasonably clean and no dog should be in a crate or pen filled with filth. The dogs themselves should look happy and healthy. You should at the very least be able to meet the mother of the litter. They may not own the father but they should be able to show you pictures at the least. You should be able to meet dogs that are related if the breeder has some in the home and the dogs should obviously be bonded to the breeder. Watch how the two interact together.

Do not be afraid to take an adult dog instead of a puppy. Adults are often fully trained which can be a blessing when you have a heavy work schedule and cannot take time off to train a puppy.

If you are at all uncomfortable, walk away. It is worth waiting for the right dog. It is better to wait for a puppy from a good breeder than to rush in and buy a puppy from the first person with one available. Waiting can save you a lot of heartache and pain, not to mention money.

Finding A Rescue Dog

Adopting a rescue dog is a great thing. There are many wonderful dogs that end up in rescue through no fault of their own. Their family may undergo a change such as a divorce and can no longer keep them or is transferred out of country. Sometimes, it is simply a matter of the wrong owner, not the wrong dog. While many rescue dogs need some training, most have no major behavioral issues. There are some that do and they need homes that are willing to work with them to overcome these problems.

When considering a rescue dog it is important to be honest with yourself about what you can and cannot deal with. It does not do the dog any good to move into your home and then have you discover that you just cannot manage him and he has to move again. Most rescue organizations are very careful about who adopts their dogs for this reason. The dog has already been through the trauma of being left once; the idea is to prevent multiple moves.

Many national clubs have links to breed rescue organizations and may even have a branch of the club devoted to rescue. They can direct you to a group in your area. Expect to fill out questionnaires and be interviewed. Unfortunately, there are some who view rescue dogs as a way to get a cheap dog that they can in turn use for criminal activity. A good rescue wants to ensure that you will give the dog the home it deserves and that your home is everything you claim. Most rescue groups conduct their interviews in your home so they can get a better feel for your suitability to a particular dog.

Unfortunately, sometimes a senior dog comes into rescue that needs a new home. Many people are leery of taking on a senior dog because the life expectancy is shorter and they may have already lost a beloved dog and be loath to go through it again too soon. Senior dogs can make great pets. Many are already trained and just looking for a nice spot to spend their final years. They may surprise you and live many more years just as some young dogs die untimely deaths due to illness. Giving them a place in your home is something you will never regret even if they are only there a short time. Rescue dogs know how to appreciate a good home because they've had the bad already. As the saying goes, "second hand dogs give first class love".

Bringing Your Puppy Home

Bringing your new dog home can be an exciting time for the whole family. Before the dog comes home, everyone should sit down together and decide on what the house rules will be. For example, will the dog be allowed on the furniture? Everyone must agree on the rules and agree to enforce them. It is very confusing for the dog if one person allows something that someone else doesn't allow.

Potty Training

Decide on where you want your dog to eliminate in your yard. Always bring him to that same spot and he will quickly pick up on where he needs to go and you will find clean up much easier. Hang a bell on the door leading to the yard. Every time you bring your puppy out to potty, gently ring the bell with their nose or paw. You want to build an association between the sound of the bell and the door opening so that your dog eventually learns to ring the bell to let you know he wants out into the yard. This helps to prevent the situation where the dog is patiently waiting at the door and no one knows he is there.

When you bring your dog out to potty he should always be on leash. This prevents him from going for a romp in the yard instead of taking care of business. Once he has eliminated, you can let him loose to have some fun while you clean up. Giving him a command as he eliminates can build an association between the act of eliminating and the word. This can be handy when travelling as some dogs can be reluctant to potty away from home. By giving the command, you are letting your pet know it is okay to eliminate in the new location.

Your puppy will always have to potty as soon as he wakes up and about twenty to thirty minutes after eating. When he is loose in your home, he should be supervised until he is housebroken. Watch for signs that he may need to potty such as circling and sniffing. Despite everyone's best efforts, accidents do occasionally happen. If you catch your puppy while he is eliminating, give him a firm no, scoop him and carry him out to wear you want him to eliminate. As soon as he goes outside, praise him lavishly for a job well done. If you discover the accident after it has occurred, there is no point in punishing your puppy. He will not know why you are upset and may even come to a seriously erroneous conclusion. Just clean the mess up and remind yourself to keep a closer eye on him next time he is loose. Most dogs have full bladder control by the time they are six months old. Until that time, accidents will occasionally occur.

Crate Training

Crate training your dog is an excellent thing to do. It will make it easier on your dog if he has to be kennelled at a boarding facility or stay overnight at the veterinarian's. It gives him a "room" of his own to retire to when he feels overwhelmed. It is also the safest way for him to travel in a vehicle and the only way an adult GSP will be travelling on an airplane.

Kennels can be wire or fibreglass. The wire ones can be preferable in a warmer climate as they allow more air flow but in the end it is mainly a personal preference and both are good. Many wire crates now come with dividers to allow you to buy a kennel that is the size you will need for your dog as an adult. You can use the dividers to make it initially smaller to accommodate a puppy and then gradually move the divider to make it bigger as he grows. In the beginning, your puppy should have enough room to lie down comfortably, have a dish and a toy and stand up without hitting his head on the top of the crate. You do not want him to have enough room to eliminate in one corner and sleep in the other. Most dogs are naturally clean and will not want to potty where they sleep. This is why crate training tends to make housetraining go faster.

A kennel is not a punishment and should never be used in that way. You want your puppy to be happy in his crate. This means doing things like having special toys for when he is in his crate such as a stuffed toy to keep him occupied. Giving him a cookie when he goes in his crate and feeding him in his kennel are other ways to make it a positive experience for him. Locate the kennel in a place with lots of foot traffic during the day such as the kitchen or living room.

The first few nights in his new home may be difficult for your puppy. He is used to sleeping with his littermates in a group and sleeping on his own may be a bit scary and lonely for him. Moving the kennel into your bedroom can help assure him that he is not alone. You need to be hard-hearted and not take him out when he cries. If you do, you will teach him that if he cries you will open the door and you will end up with a dog that understands how to push your buttons and get exactly what he wants, and you will regret it. You will quickly learn to distinguish between a cry that means "I need to potty" and one that means "I want out". If in doubt, take the puppy out to potty and then immediately return him to his crate. He will quickly learn the routine.

Because the crate is your dog's room, it should be respected as his sanctuary. You should be able to take anything out that you wish, but when he goes there voluntarily, respect that and let him be alone.

Pet Insurance

Sooner or later the odds are good that your pet will have an injury or illness that requires veterinary care. If you are good at setting money aside for a rainy day, then it is wise to open a savings account into which you regularly deposit funds for potential vet bills. If you are not good at saving money, you may be better to look into purchasing pet insurance.

If you decide to get pet insurance, it is important to read the fine print carefully and look at a variety of different plans and companies before making your decision. Like any other type of insurance, some plans are better than others.

Socialization

A good breeder begins socializing their puppies from a young age. They expose them to different surfaces to walk on, items to play with, people to meet, etc. Once your puppy comes home with you, that responsibility falls onto your shoulders. At a young age, dogs, like children, are less frightened of the world and more open to learning and experiencing new things. It is during this time that you want to expose your dog to as many situations, people, and other animals as possible without overwhelming him. It can be a fine line. Signing up for a puppy socialization class can be a good first step. Discuss where you can safely take your new puppy in your region. In some areas, diseases like parvovirus are prevalent and young puppies should avoid areas where they may be exposed to the disease. This is something your veterinarian can advise you on.

You can introduce you new puppy to dogs that you know are fully vaccinated such as those of friends and family members. Try to take him places like your local pet supply store where he will meet strangers of all ages as well as other pets.

Dogs can go through a fear period between 12-16 weeks and during this time they can easily be frightened of unusual or strange things they have not previously been exposed to. Socializing from a young age can make this period easier. Like people, the older dogs get the less most of them like change.

Dog Sports

The German shorthaired pointer is an active and athletic dog which makes a good candidate for many dog sports. There are a number of sports offered by national clubs like the American Kennel Club (AKC) through which you can earn titles and, more importantly, have a lot of fun with your dog.

Agility

Agility is kind of like a timed obstacle course for your dog. You, the handler, run alongside and direct him towards each obstacle in a specific order. Common obstacles include A-frames, teeter totters, tunnels, jumps, and weave poles. Agility is a great way to build confidence in a more timid dog. It's also a lot of fun and a great way to burn off a GSP's energy.

Obedience

There is the traditional form of obedience that most people are familiar with, but there is also a newer type of obedience called rally. The newer form is more relaxed and puts more focus on the relationship between the handler and the dog, rather than the minute precision of the exercises being performed. Most of the exercises are the same for both of them. In rally, the judge lays out a course with signs indicating which exercise should be performed where. The handler guides their dog through the course and, unlike traditional obedience, is allowed to provide verbal encouragement. It is rapidly gaining in popularity.

Dock Dogs

This is a sport that is perfect for a dog that loves the water. There are three basic types of events. Big Air is basically a long jump into the pool off of a dock. Extreme Vertical is a high jump event. A bumper is suspended above the water, and raised in two inch intervals at each level. Speed Retrieve involves a timed swim to the end of the pool to retrieve a toy. Dogs competing in all three events are known as Iron Dog triathlon competitors and the dog with the highest combined score from all three events wins that competition.

Conformation

Conformation showing is a sport. It was designed to evaluate the structure and features of breeding stock to determine which dog best fits the breed standard. Many people mistake it for a beauty pageant, but when done correctly it is not that at all. Body structure including bone lengths and angulation, is very important to how a dog does his original job. A poorly constructed dog is less likely to be able to do his job successfully over the course of his lifetime because the body wears down and becomes more prone to injuries. In extreme cases, he may not be able to do his job at all.

If you are interested in conformation showing, you should discuss it with the breeder of your dog to ensure that you get a puppy suitable for the show ring. If you wish to show the dog yourself, you should consider signing up for conformation handling classes so you can learn what is expected of you and your dog in the ring. You can also choose to hire a professional handler to show your dog for you if you would prefer to watch from outside the ring.

Breeding Your Dog & Puppy Development

The decision to breed your dog should not be made lightly. There are many dogs in need of homes and a good breeder needs to take responsibility for the dogs he produces for the rest of their life. This means that if their owner cannot keep them, regardless of the age of the dog or reason they are giving them up, the responsible breeder will take them back and keep them until a new home can be found for the dog. Shelters are full of unwanted dogs with bad breeders. If you do not intend to take the responsibility seriously and stand behind the dogs you produce, then do everyone a favour and spay your female.

Breeding dogs can be very expensive. Good breeders seldom make money and more often than not, they lose money. It can also be heartbreaking. Your girl may die due to complications in the birthing process. Puppies do not always thrive and you may find that one or more of the puppies in the litter die within the first few weeks of birth. Showing your children the miracle of life is not a good reason to breed your dog unless you also want to show them the tragedy of death. There are much better ways to educate your children about life and death than breeding your dog.

Finding homes for puppies is not always easy either. You may end up with half the litter not sold at eight weeks of age. Ten GSPs that are eight weeks of age are a lot of work. Even if half are sold, you will still have five to look after. Those five will need to be socialized and trained. That's a lot of work. Some people still have puppies in need of homes at six months of age. Do you have the room to care for the dogs for that long?

Mentors

If you are serious about breeding and are not to be dissuaded, you should sit down with the breeder of your dog and discuss it. They can advise you on what needs to be done, what lines will work best with theirs, choosing a stud dog, etc. Most breeders place their dogs on non-breeding contracts that can only be lifted if you meet certain conditions such as having the appropriate health testing done.

If you have never whelped a litter before, you should make sure you have someone experienced on hand for the birth of your puppies. They are more likely to recognize signs of difficulty or distress that indicate your girl should be brought to a veterinarian as soon as possible. They will also be more prepared for the care of the puppies and able to advise you on what you need to do. It is not something you can learn in a book and having a mentor to guide you is important to ensuring that your girl and the puppies survive your learning curve.

Puppies at Birth

When the puppies are born they will be blind and their ears will be closed. Their bodies do not regulate temperature very well initially and they must be kept warm. If they get chilled, they may die. The tails must be docked and dewclaws removed within the first few days of life. If you have someone experienced willing to help that will work. If not, ask your veterinarian to do it for you.

When GSP puppies are born only the patches and solid colours are in place; the rest of the body is white with no ticking. The ticking will come in gradually as they age.

The mother produces a special substance in her milk known as colostrum in the first 24 hours after birth. Colostrum helps pass the mother's immunity on to her puppies. It is very important that they get it. If they cannot nurse due to a problem with the mother, you will need to purchase artificial colostrum through your veterinarian.

Weigh the puppies daily and keep track of their weight. Although they may lose a touch in the first day or two, they should gain steadily after that. Well fed, healthy puppies do a lot of sleeping and eating in the first few weeks. Puppies that are crying in the whelping box are hungry and need to be cared for by you. While many dogs take naturally to motherhood, not all do and if your girl doesn't than you need to fill in for her. You will need to rub genitals to ensure that they eliminate and takeover feeding duties. Puppies eat frequently so be prepared for very little sleep and several weeks off work until they can be introduced to food in a pan at about two weeks.

The First Four Weeks

During those initial two weeks, the puppies are fragile. They are easily chilled and diarrhea can dehydrate them very quickly. Most things that will go wrong will happen during this period of time. By ten to fourteen days, their eyes and ears begin to open. The eyes are initially blue and darken as they age. By the time they go home they are usually hazel in colour and will darken to brown in coming months. They stumble around the box on wobbly legs and begin to become quite cute.

Provided that everything goes well and your girl has been an exemplary mother, there isn't a lot for you to do in those first few weeks other than hover and worry. As they get older though, their mother will begin to cede duties like cleaning up after them and feeding them to you.

From Four Weeks Onward

Puppies can be started on food in many different ways. One of the most common is to combine goat's milk and pablum with ground up dog food to create a mush. Goat's milk has less lactose and is easier for puppies to digest than cow's milk. As they continue to grow they will also begin to play with one another and you. Their personalities begin to emerge between three and four weeks of age. Now the real work begins.

By this time, many mothers are more than happy to let you do all the cleaning and most of the feeding. It's a full time job with a big litter and the average litter size in German shorthaired pointers is 8-10 puppies with some litters being as large as 15 pups. It is between four and eight weeks that they begin to develop canine social skills for interacting with other dogs. Puppies taken away from their littermates too soon, as often happens with puppies sold through pet stores, lose out on valuable learning skills which will allow them to understand canine body language and learn to play and interact with other dogs.

This is also the time when you need to begin socializing the litter. They need to be exposed to new items, new surfaces to walk on, lots of people, household noises, etc. Your puppy buyers will want to come and meet the puppies. They will not want to see shy puppies. They want to see happy, healthy, playful and confident little dogs. It is your job to ensure that that is exactly what they do see by making sure your pups are well socialized.

Photo Credits

Name   Pages

Heather Brennan – 12, 15, 30, 37, 82, 92, 94, 102, 108, 109, 112, 114

Joanna Brennan – 83

Kelly Elson – 18, 49, 58, 62

Flying High K9s – 35, 50, 76, 105, 106

Rene Jones – 10, 103

Norman LeCouvie – 104

Mike Milton – 9, 20

Kerry Murray – 61

Andrew Phillips – 36

Sarah Struetta – 89

Index

Adoption – 68, 87, 93, 95
Agility – 18, 22, 23, 34, 104
American Kennel Club (AKC) - 21, 22, 34, 51, 57, 60, 101
Animal rights activists – 39
Big Air – 106
Black GSP – 17, 27, 31, 33-36
Bonding with people – 75, 85, 93
Breed standards and practices – 18, 21, 34, 35, 107
Breeders – 5, 11,17, 19, 21, 28, 33, 34, 40, 59, 81, 83, 84, 89-93, 101, 107, 109, 110
Breeding – 5, 17, 21, 22, 61, 63, 82, 89, 105, 110
Canadian Kennel Club (CKC) – 22, 51
Cancer – 84
Children – 13, 14, 66, 101, 110
Ciro v Bichtelwald - 35
Colostrum – 111, 112
Colour – 17, 21, 29, 33, 34, 36, 47, 71, 73, 111, 113
Commands – 76-79, 98
Conformation 21, 22, 34, 35, 91, 106, 107
Crate training – 98, 99
Dayblindness (CD) – 79, 83, 91
Deutsch Kurzhaar (DK) – 9, 61, 62
Dewclaw – 27, 39, 111
Diseases – 81-84, 86, 91, 101
Disqualifications – 29, 31, 34
Dock dogs – 18, 106
Docking – 39, 40
Dog sport – 18, 21, 103-107
Drop ear – 72
English pointer – 16, 17, 33, 43
Epilepsy 84
Extreme Vertical - 106
Eye Disease – 79, 81, 83, 91
Eyes – 22, 24, 31, 50, 59, 81, 91, 113
FCI standard – 22, 23, 25, 34

Field test – 34, 57, 58
Field trial – 21, 34, 51, 57-59
Flushing – 15, 16, 43, 46, 51, 54
Food – 13, 53, 68, 75, 76, 112, 113
Foot hunter – 11, 57, 59
Forequarters – 27
Gait – 30
Game – 10, 15-19, 25, 26, 43, 50, 51
Genetics – 11, 36, 81, 90
German wirehaired pointer – 10, 44, 46
Germans – 16, 17, 33, 34
Grooming – 65, 67, 71
Gun dogs – 16, 21, 30, 51, 59
Gun – 16, 53-55
Gunshyness – 53
Hindquarters - 28
Hip Dysplasia – 82
Hunt point retrieve (HPR) dogs - 19
Hunting -
Hypothyroidism
Iron Dog – 106
KS Zobel v Pregelufer - 35
Leash – 65, 66, 68, 76-79, 97
Litter – 36, 41, 89, 93, 110-115
Lupoid Dermatosis (LD) – 84
Muzzle- 25,46
NAVHDA – 45, 47
Neck – 26, 27
Noblemen -15
Nutrition – 68
Obedience – 34, 75, 104, 105
Pasterns – 27
PennHIP – 82, 83
Personality -66, 69
Pet – 9, 11-13, 18, 40, 49, 65-68, 73, 75, 90, 96, 98, 100-102

Pet Insurance – 100, 101
Pointing – 16, 21, 27, 45, 47, 49, 54, 57
Potty training – 97, 98
    Proportion – 23-26
    Prussian shorthairs – 17, 33
    Puppies – 21, 36, 39, 40, 53, 54, 59, 65, 66, 68, 75, 77, 78, 81, 84, 91-93, 97-102, 107, 109-115
    Quartering field – 45, 46, 49
    Registration – 17, 33, 34, 61-63
    Rescue dog – 12, 89, 95, 96
    Schweisshunde – 16
Separation anxiety – 85-87
    Setters – 10, 17, 43-46
    Shedding – 71
    Show dog – 18, 91, 107
    Size – 9, 22-24, 35
    Socialization – 75, 99, 115
    Speed Retrieve – 106
    Subaortic Stenosis – 81, 82
    Temperament – 31
    Torn Cruciate – 84
    Training – 13, 49, 51, 65, 66, 75, 76, 79, 93, 95-99, 110
Versatile hunting dogs – 10, 16, 21, 43-47
Vizsla – 10, 44, 46
    Wall eyes – 24, 31
    Weimaraner – 10, 43, 46

Resources

Reference Books

<u>Der Deutsch Kurzhaar</u> by Georgina Byrne

<u>The New German Shorthaired Pointer</u> by C. Bede Maxwell

Club Websites

German Shorthaired Pointer Club of America – gspca.org

German Shorthaired Pointer Club of Canada – gspcanada.com

The German Shorthaired Pointer Club (UK) – www.gsp.org.uk

The German Shorthaired Pointer International Club (UK) – gspic.webs.com

German Shorthaired Pointer Club of Western Australia – gspwa.net

German Shorthaired Pointer Club of Victora – gspvic.org.au

German Shorthaired Club of Southern Australia – gspclubsa.com

Made in the USA
San Bernardino, CA
16 December 2014